The Country Set

Hannah Dale

The Country Set

Hannah Dale

BATSFORD

For Amelia, Lara and Oliver

First published in the United Kingdom in 2014 by
National Trust Books

This edition first published in 2017 by
Batsford
43 Great Ormond Street
London WC1N 3HZ

An imprint of Pavilion Books Group Ltd

ISBN: 9781909881037

A CIP catalogue record for this book is available from
the British Library.

20 19 18
10 9

Reproduction by Mission Production Ltd, Hong Kong
Printed and bound by Toppan Leefung Printing Ltd, China

This book can be ordered direct from the publisher at the website
www.pavilionbooks.com, or try your local bookshop.

Contents

Introduction

I'm currently sitting at my desk by the window, hoping for a
sudden bolt of creative inspiration to strike and wondering how
I can possibly distil a subject as broad and wonderful as 'British
Wildlife' into a mere introduction. It is a grey January day and
despite the bare, damp trees and empty, rather sad-looking
flowerbeds, I can see a handsome cock pheasant stalking slowly
through the undergrowth, the glint of his head like a green
jewel against the brown and grey background. An inquisitive
robin is hopping along a stretch of trellis and I marvel at his
ability to make a living when everything looks so bleak. A lone
rabbit ambles through the flowerbed in search of any green
shoots and I just see the flash of his white tail as he disappears
under the fence. And there it is; inspiration. We are so lucky
to be surrounded by such a diverse abundance of wildlife in
Britain, from the remarkable barn owl that can detect and
locate its prey from the tiniest sound in the undergrowth, to the
sociable otter making a game of sliding down riverbanks on his
belly. Did you know that the little wren's voice is ten times
louder than that of a cockerel, weight for weight? Or that the
clever magpie can count? I find it fascinating to see how
evolution has shaped the characteristics of each and every
animal to be perfectly suited to its environment, and how
adaptable they are. Many species have learned to live happily

alongside us in our ever-changing world and even in the cities there is an abundance of life if you know where to look.

I first discovered my love of drawing and painting wildlife while studying for a degree in Zoology at Cambridge University. As well as fuelling my fascination for animals and their behaviour, I was lucky enough to get involved in various fieldwork projects, studying species in their natural habitats. One such project was looking at bowerbirds in Queensland, Australia. These fascinating birds build elaborate bowers to attract potential mates, and during one observation sitting, I happened to take a sketchbook. I had always loved drawing and painting and I took so much pleasure from sketching the birds and animals that came into my field of view, capturing something of their character and personality.

After a stint in London, I picked up my paintbrushes again a few years later when I settled back in my home county of Lincolnshire with my husband, Jack, and our three young children. We keep chickens and I began sketching them pecking around our garden – I particularly love drawing birds; they have so much character, which I always try to capture in my paintings. Looking at their bony beaks and scaly feet, I am always reminded of the dinosaurs from which they evolved. One of my favourite subjects is guinea fowl – they are so expressive with their long eyelashes and raucous nature!

I feel incredibly privileged to live surrounded by British countryside and farmland and am constantly inspired by our wild neighbours – from the Mad March hares with their characterful faces and gentle personalities to the charming pheasants, strutting wildly across the road. This book provides a small snapshot of some of Britain's most well-loved wildlife. I hope that the illustrations capture something of the essence of the wonderful personalities we share our world with and, above all, inspire you to celebrate the great British countryside.

Woodland

Hedgehog
Erinaceus europaeus

The hedgehog is undoubtedly one of Britain's most appealing and popular characters, even appearing in Shakespeare's *The Tempest* and *A Midsummer Night's Dream*, referred to as hedgepigs or urchins. An average adult hedgehog is covered with 5,000–7,000 spines, protecting it from predation. They are well adapted to urban environments and make themselves at home in our gardens, often visiting up to ten gardens on their nocturnal travels.

Badger
Meles meles

The badger, with its characteristic black- and white-striped face, is a well-loved countryside character. With short, powerful limbs and strong claws, it is well adapted for digging its underground burrows or setts. Badgers are very clean animals and make excellent housekeepers, regularly changing their dirty bedding. They are also generally very peaceful animals and have been known to share their burrows with other species, such as foxes or rabbits. Badgers appear frequently in folklore and literature, particularly in children's fiction, perhaps this is a reason for our enduring affection for these iconic animals.

Tawny Owl
Strix aluco

The tawny owl is one of our most familiar owls. It is a stealthy and silent nocturnal hunter, relying on its excellent hearing, which is ten times better than human hearing, to detect the smallest movements of prey in the distant undergrowth. Tawny owls nest in holes in trees and will fiercely defend their young, but chase the fledglings from their territory after the breeding season. Consequently, the mortality rate of young owls is high. Tawny owls have long been the subject of superstitions, and are thought by some to be an omen of bad luck.

Red Squirrel
Sciurus vulgaris

The iconic red squirrel, with its copper pelt and tufty ears, is a much-loved British native. The familiar bushy tail is used for balance and steering while jumping from tree to tree and is also thought to keep them warm at night. The name 'squirrel' even comes from the Greek for 'shade-tailed'. In addition to their treetop acrobatics, Red squirrels are also excellent swimmers. They are famed for burying caches of nuts and seeds for the lean winter months, but their memory is not as good as that of grey squirrels, and they often forget where they have buried their stash. Most of Britain's red squirrels are now found in Scotland.

Little Owl
Athene noctua

The little owl, as the name suggests, is our smallest owl, measuring just 22cm (8½in). It was introduced into Britain in the nineteenth century but has quickly made itself at home and is in fact one of the most widely distributed owls globally, partly due to its ability to live happily alongside humans. Although the little owl mainly hunts at night, it can often be seen perching on posts or branches during the day, bobbing its head up and down. The little owl was associated with Athena, the Greek goddess of wisdom, hence its genus name, *Athene*.

Red Deer
Cervus elaphus

Red deer are the fourth largest deer species on the planet and our largest land mammal. They live in hierarchical groups with the stags all striving to be the alpha male. During the breeding season, they perform the annual rut where testosterone-charged males size one another up, often resulting in a clashing of antlers that can cause serious injury. The male sheds his antlers annually and they regrow each spring, at a rate of up to 2.5cm (1in) per day. The antlers regrow larger each year with more tines, so the oldest males have the most impressive antlers.

Great Spotted Woodpecker
Dendrocopos major

The great spotted woodpecker can be found in woodlands and sometimes in parks, although it will occasionally make its way to our bird tables, reportedly being partial to peanuts in particular. More commonly, it is reliant on old, decaying trees for food and nesting locations. Despite its dramatic colouring, the great spotted woodpecker is more often heard than seen, heralding its presence with a rhythmic drumming as it pounds its beak on branches or tree trunks. The great spotted woodpecker's skull is a remarkable feat of engineering, enabling it to slam its beak into wood at 1,000 times the force of gravity, with no trace of a headache!

Fox

Vulpes vulpes

The beautiful red fox is well known for its intelligence and
adaptability. Traditionally found in the countryside, foxes
have more recently made themselves at home in our towns
and cities, where they thrive alongside humans, and can
often be seen in our gardens. Hunting at night, they have
excellent night vision and their eyes will appear bright
green if a light is shined on them in the dark. Foxes are
very vocal and can often be heard barking and calling to
one another – in fact, twelve different types of sound
have been identified in adults.

Grey Squirrel
Sciurus carolinensis

The grey squirrel is very common across much of Britain,
having been introduced from America in the nineteenth
century. It has earned a bad reputation for its effect on
the numbers of our native red squirrel, as it is better
adapted and more resistant to disease than its red cousins.
The grey squirrel has an excellent memory and hoards
food for the winter months. The clever little rodent has
even been known to trick observers by pretending to bury
its food while hiding it in its mouth and then taking it
to a more private location.

Dormouse

Muscardinus avellanarius

The dormouse is a golden coloured, mouse-like rodent
with a bushy tail and black beady eyes. It lives in trees and
hedgerows, particularly favouring hazel, and feeds on seeds,
berries and insects. The dormouse's Latin name
avellanarius means 'hazel'. As immortalised in Lewis
Carroll's *Alice's Adventures in Wonderland*, the sleepy
dormouse is one of only three British mammals to truly
hibernate. The name 'dormouse' even derives from the
French 'dormir', meaning to sleep.

Common Shrew

Sorex araneus

The busy little common shrew, with its pointy, mobile snout is always on the go, and needs to eat every two to three hours as it can die of starvation after only five hours without food. It is active both day and night, taking only short rests between bursts of activity. The common shrew's tiny eyes have poor vision, but it uses smell and sound to locate its food. It is easily startled and often faints or has even been known to drop dead at a sudden noise.

Stoat
Mustela erminea

The stoat, despite its relatively small size and dainty
appearance is a very effective predator, hunting mainly
rodents but also rabbits and even the occasional brown
hare. It was introduced to New Zealand to help control the
rabbit population but had a devastating effect on their
native birds. Its sandy fur moults as the weather cools, and
the stoat then sports its winter coat, pristine white except
for the black tail. The opportunistic stoat doesn't build
its own den but adds insult to injury by hijacking the
burrows of its recently devoured prey.

Fallow Deer
Dama dama

The beautiful fallow deer has to be one of our most attractive mammals, with its spotted flanks and flattened antlers. It likes to live in woodlands but will also enjoy grazing in open areas as long as there is some woodland cover nearby. It is a shy animal but is surprisingly abundant and causes something of a nuisance by grazing on young tree shoots and agricultural crops.

Barn Owl
Tyto alba

The pale barn owl with its long legs and wings, and
distinctive heart-shaped face, is one of Britain's most
popular birds. It doesn't hoot like other owls, but makes
a shrill, screeching sound. The barn owl hunts silently at
night, preying on voles and mice that it detects scurrying
around in the undergrowth with its excellent hearing;
barn owls do not rely on sight to hunt at all. The supply
of voles determines how many eggs the female will lay
each year. Chicks in the nest have occasionally been
observed to feed one another – this sign of sibling
affection is very unusual in birds.

Mole

Talpa europaea

A mole's presence is usually signalled by tell-tale mounds of earth from its excavated burrows, often protruding from an otherwise manicured lawn. As a result, the mole is an unpopular visitor for many gardeners. Spending most of its life underground, the mole has poor eyesight but what it lacks in this department it makes up for in its digging ability, with large paws and even an extra thumb to help shift more soil. The mole's favourite food is worms, and it must eat every few hours or it will die. It has underground larders where it stores caches of worms for later consumption.

Farmland

Red-legged Partridge
Alectoris rufa

The round-bodied, red-legged partridge was introduced to Britain as a game bird but it has made itself at home in our countryside. It is a sociable bird and can often be seen in large family groups that make a striking sight with their distinctive markings and characteristic red legs. Although red-legged partridges prefer to run, they will fly over short distances, with their small rounded wings making a soft whirring sound. Unusually, the female occasionally lays two separate clutches of eggs – she will incubate one set herself, while putting the dedicated father to work incubating the second set.

Rabbit
Oryctolagus cuniculus

Loved and loathed in equal measure, the rabbit is one of
Britain's most sociable mammals, living in underground
warrens in groups of two to ten individuals. Originating in
Southern Europe and thought to have been introduced to
Britain by the Romans, the humble bunny has made its
presence felt in most parts of the world, largely due to its
infamous reproductive capability. One pair of rabbits can
produce 30–40 offspring in a year, and this has meant that
rabbits have become quite a pest in many places, causing
damage to native wildlife and vegetation. However, all
breeds of domestic rabbit descend from the wild rabbit,
and make one of our best-loved childhood pets.

Kestrel

Falco tinnunculus

The kestrel is one of our smallest and most abundant birds of prey. It can be recognised in flight by the long wings and characteristic long tail. It hunts in open spaces, hovering 10–20m above the ground and using its excellent eyesight to spot small movements of prey. Mice and voles make up the majority of the kestrel's diet, but it will also take small birds and has been known to steal prey from sparrowhawks or owls. Adding to its reputation for thievery, the kestrel doesn't build its own nest either, but will often borrow old pigeon or sparrowhawk nests.

Pheasant
Phasianus colchicus

Although a quintessential symbol of the British countryside, the handsome pheasant with his chestnut, gold body and iridescent green head, is native to Asia, and was introduced to Britain as a game bird. It is commercially bred across the country and is one of the world's most hunted birds.

Commonly found in open countryside, woodland, hedgerows and coppices, the pheasant feeds on the ground but likes to roost in the trees. Although it can fly, it prefers to run, and can reach speeds close to 16km/h (10 mph).

Brown Hare

Lepus europaeus

The brown hare is very much loved in Britain and, with its
long legs and large ears, it is often viewed as a symbol of the
countryside. Our ancestors also appear to have shared our
fascination with this gentle creature and it symbolised
fertility and reproduction in Pagan culture. Usually a shy
animal, brown hares well and truly come out of their shells
in the springtime and the 'Mad March hares' can be seen
tearing after one another in open countryside. The iconic
boxing brown hares were once thought to be males
fighting over females, but it is now believed these eccentric
displays are usually a female hare hitting a male.

Lapwing

Vanellus vanellus

The lapwing, easily recognised by the characteristic plume on its head, is also known as a 'peewit' which is a good imitation of its shrill cry. A very social bird, the lapwing migrates in large, noisy flocks. In Britain, it is commonly found in open arable farmland and as a ground nesting bird, lays its eggs in scraped-out hollows. The females noisily and aggressively defend their young from predators. The name 'lapwing' is thought to come from the lapping sound the wings make when the males perform their erratic, tumbling display flights – they make quite a sight.

Harvest Mouse
Micromys minutus

The harvest mouse is Britain's smallest rodent, weighing
only as much as a 20p piece, and makes its home in fields
of cereal crops and other tall vegetation, such as reed
beds and hedgerows. Its Latin name means 'smallest tiny
mouse'. The agile little harvest mouse uses its prehensile tail
as an extra limb, helping it to navigate its way through the
forests of corn in which it lives. It is also a skilled
weaver, crafting a spherical nest above the ground,
5–10 cm (2–4in) in diameter.

Barn Swallow
Hirundo rustica

The barn swallow is one of our most recognisable and well-loved birds with a deep, forked tail and distinctive red and blue colouring. It has long been the symbol of safe return for mariners (hence often appearing in tattoos), and has graced the pages of many works of literature, from the Bible to Shakespeare and Keats. The barn swallow is most famous for its winter migrations to Africa, Arabia and the Indian Sub-continent. During these hazardous journeys, the barn swallow covers distances of up to 322km (200 miles) a day. From May to September, it resides in Britain, feeding on insects plucked from the sky during aerial hunts, and drinking water obtained by skimming over lakes with an open mouth.

Rivers and Ponds

Otter

Lutra lutra

One of our top predators, the otter hunts fish, small
waterbirds, amphibians and crustaceans. It is well adapted to
an aquatic habitat, with webbed feet and dense fur, as well as
having ears and nostrils that it can close when underwater.
Otters can remain submerged for up to four minutes while
they are diving. They are also very sociable and playful
animals, making them very popular with nature lovers.
They can often be seen sliding down banks and hills on
their bellies, or play fighting with one another.

Mallard

Anas platyrhynchos

The mallard is Britain's most common and easily
recognisable duck, as it is widely spread across the UK.
Hugely adaptable, it lives happily alongside humans and
thrives in the ponds and rivers of urban areas. The male has
a characteristic iridescent green head and white collar, but
loses his fine feathers during the winter moult, when he
looks more like the brown, mottled female. The female is a
lot noisier than the male, making the familiar loud quacking
noise. The males are much more softly spoken. Most breeds
of domestic duck descend from the mallard.

Mute Swan
Cygnus olor

The mute swan is one of our largest birds, the males
weighing a whopping 13kg (28lb). Mute swans are often
associated with romance as they mate for life and
frequently return to the same nest site year after year.
They build large nests on islands in lakes or close to lake
edges and are famous for aggressively defending their
young. Their powerful wings are anecdotally said to be
strong enough to break a man's arm with one swipe. A swan
used to be the centrepiece of many royal banquets and the
British monarch still retains the right to ownership of all
swans. The tradition of 'Swan Upping', an annual census of
the number of swans on stretches of the River Thames and
its tributaries, still takes place each year.

Canada Goose
Branta canadensis

The Canada goose was introduced from North America in the seventeenth century, but this attractive goose is now resident across most of the UK, and its success has led to it being seen as a pest in some areas. It is a migratory bird and forms the striking V-shaped formation during flight. With a wing span of over 1.8m (6ft), it can reach astonishing speeds of 97km/h (60mph) an hour.

Moorhen
Gallinula chloropus

The moorhen is a striking bird with jet black plumage,
a red beak and yellow legs, ending in long toes that it uses
to walk over floating vegetation. The moorhen lives
around fresh or brackish waters and is a good swimmer,
despite not possessing webbed feet. It can sometimes be
seen lifting its legs out of the water in front of its body
as it swims, in a rather comic manner, supposedly to
lift them over vegetation. The moorhen is also
colourfully known as the 'swamp chicken'.

Grey Heron
Ardea cinerea

The grey heron is a tall wading bird, standing at around a metre tall, but with a wingspan of up to 1.8m (6ft). It mainly feeds on fish, but will also eat small mammals, birds, reptiles and amphibians. It is a cunning predator, waiting silently or slowly stalking its victims. It is also very adaptable and can often be spotted at penguin or seal enclosures during feeding time at zoos, waiting for an opportunity to steal a fish. Owners of fish ponds are always wary of marauding grey herons, but they are very difficult to deter – plastic decoys tend to attract rather than discourage them! They are sociable birds, nesting in large heronries in the treetops which can contain hundreds of individual nests.

Kingfisher
Alcedo atthis

With its vivid, iridescent feathers and bright colouring, the kingfisher is one of our most recognisable birds. You are most likely to see a flash of blue and orange as this little bird darts around alongside rivers or lakes. The kingfisher needs to eat 60 per cent of its body weight in fish each day so it is perfectly adapted for fishing. It has a third eyelid which protects its eyes underwater, enabling it to see its prey, and a streamlined beak for spearing fish. The male courts the female by offering her a fish supper. If he can't tempt her, the amorous suitor eats the fish himself. The female lays her eggs in a burrow, which the male and female laboriously excavate in sandy riverbanks.

Water Vole
Arvicola amphibius

The water vole, with its chubby face and round nose was
immortalised as 'Ratty' in Kenneth Grahame's *Wind in the
Willows*. It is a shy and secretive little rodent, and makes its
home in networks of burrows along riverbanks and lakes,
or will sometimes build nests in reed beds if no suitable
bank is available. The water vole is an accomplished
swimmer and escapes predators underwater by kicking
up a cloud of mud from the river bed – obscuring the
pursuer's vision while the agile vole makes its escape.

Greylag Goose
Anser anser

The greylag goose is Britain's native goose species and is the ancestor of most species of domestic goose. They tend to be amongst the last birds to migrate, and some suggest that this is the reason for the 'lag' in their name. They have a loud, distinctive honking voice and mate for life. If separated, they call out to one another and, rather touchingly, after being separated from their mate for any length of time, they perform a courtship ritual on being reunited.

Common Frog

Rana temporaria

The common frog is an amphibious resident of our ponds
and rivers. Famous for its metamorphic life cycle, it is a
favourite with children and the appearance of frogspawn is a
sure sign that spring is on its way. The common frog uses its
skin to breathe and mustn't allow it to dry out, so is usually
found close to a water source, hiding (or hibernating in
winter) in a damp spot amongst leaves or rotting tree
stumps. Its eyes and nostrils are located at the top of its
head, allowing it to be concealed from predators under the
water while being able to see and breathe at the same time.

Common Toad
Bufo bufo

Perhaps because of its warty appearance or because it tends to crawl and creep out of dark hiding places, the common toad has long been associated with bad luck and witchcraft. It spends much of the year hidden away amongst fallen leaves, tree roots or between rocks, seeking the company of other toads only during the mating season. Glands in the common toad's skin secrete a foul-tasting substance that prevents other animals from wanting to eat it. In 2007, cameras were sent to the bottom of Loch Ness in search of the proverbial monster. No monster was seen, but the researchers were surprised to see toads walking along the bottom of the Loch, 99m (325ft) down!

Sea and Coastline

Puffin
Fratercula arctica

The 'clown of the sea' is a striking bird with its bright
orange legs and broad, brightly coloured beak, perfectly
adapted to catching fish. Its Latin name means 'friar',
a reference to its black and white plumage, resembling
the colours of a monk's robes. The puffin spends most
of its time fishing out in the open ocean, but returns to
the coastline to breed. Nesting colonies of puffins
encrusting the clifftops make quite a striking impact.
They build networks of burrows in which to lay their
eggs, and as creatures of habit, each year they like
to return to the same burrow.

Herring Gull
Larus argentatus

The raucous and riotous herring gull is an iconic bird of
our coastline. With its noisy laughter and large size, it has
gained something of a bad reputation. It is a confident bird
and happily lives alongside humans, and is notorious for
stealing chips from holiday-makers in our seaside towns.
However, as a scavenger, it is one of nature's cleaners,
mopping up waste and detritus and keeping rat numbers
down by taking food before the rats have the opportunity
to do so. Herring gulls can often be seen performing a
bizarre dance, drumming their feet on the ground.
This is to encourage worms to the surface, which
they promptly devour.

Grey Seal

Halichoerus grypus

The grey seal's Latin name means 'hook-nosed sea pig' but despite this rather unflattering title, the intelligent grey seal is rather endearing and large breeding colonies along our coastline in the autumn draw huge crowds of tourists. The grey seal is superbly adapted to catching fish and has good eyesight for spotting prey in the murky water, but also has excellent hearing and sensitive whiskers that help it to catch its supper. It can dive for up to 16 minutes under water and the thick insulating blubber and waterproof fur enable it to survive in water that would kill humans in minutes.

Garden and
Meadow

Blue Tit
Cyanistes caeruleus

The cheeky blue tit is easily recognised by its striking yellow plumage and blue cap. The brightness of its yellow breast is determined by the abundance of green caterpillars, a favourite food of the blue tit. The agile little bird is known for its treetop gymnastics, clinging to the smallest of branches or hanging upside down in the pursuit of food. It is an intelligent bird and if you still have your milk delivered, you may notice the foil top has been pecked away by an opportunistic blue tit in search of a creamy snack.

Chaffinch
Fringilla coelebs

The rusty coloured chaffinch has long been prized for its melodious song. In Victorian times, chaffinches were kept as pets and made to compete in singing contests with other captive birds. A prolific male chaffinch can repeat his song up to 3,000 times a day and chaffinches are also known to have different regional accents. They are often seen in large male-only flocks, hence their Latin name *coelebs*, meaning 'bachelor'.

Wren

Troglodytes troglodytes

The wren is one of our smallest birds and appeared on the
smallest British coin, the farthing. The Latin name *troglodytes*
means 'cave dweller' and refers to the wren's habit of
creeping into little nooks and crannies to roost or to wait
for passing insects. The wren has a very loud voice despite
its diminutive size. Weight for weight, its voice is ten times
louder than that of a cockerel. A sociable little bird, wrens
like to roost together in the winter and up to 60 have been
spotted in a single nest box.

Magpie

Pica pica

The black and white magpie has earned itself a bad reputation as a thief, said to have a penchant for shiny objects. It is also unpopular for its habit of raiding eggs from the nests of songbirds and the effects this is thought to have had on their population numbers. However, it is one of the most highly intelligent of all birds, and even of all living creatures. Its talents include tool use, elaborate social rituals and even counting. It is also the subject of many superstitions, and the number of magpies seen is said to predict the future in the nursery rhyme 'one for sorrow'.

House Sparrow
Passer domesticus

The noisy house sparrow is one of our most sociable birds,
roosting in large groups in shrubs and hedges. It can often
be seen taking dust or water baths with its pals, and is also
very happy in the company of humans, usually living in close
proximity to people. Sparrow pie used to be a favourite dish
across Europe and was thought to have aphrodisiac
properties, probably because of the prolific reproductive
capability of the cheeky house sparrow.

Goldfinch
Carduelis carduelis

The goldfinch is a small and dainty bird but its striking colouring makes it one of the most attractive to grace our gardens. Quite appropriately, the collective noun for goldfinches is a 'charm'. They are very sociable birds and form large flocks after the breeding season, sometimes containing thousands of individuals. Goldfinches are famous for their love of thistle seeds, but if you wish to attract them to your bird table, keeping it well stocked with nyjer seeds is a good idea as these are another goldfinch favourite.

Great Tit
Parus major

Great tits are easily recognisable from their yellow front and black caps. They have a huge song vocabulary and female great tits prefer to choose mates with the widest variety of songs. Great tits are intelligent little birds and are adept at using tools, for example, using a twig to retrieve an insect from a hole in a tree. Great tits like woodland environments and nest in cavities, such as hollow tree trunks, but are very versatile and happily use garden nest boxes. They have even been known to nest in postboxes!

Blackbird

Turdus merula

The blackbird is Britain's most abundant bird and is often a
frequent visitor to our gardens. Its song is perhaps one of
the most familiar and can be heard between January and
July. It is said that the blackbird's favourite time to sing is
after it has rained. Blackbirds mate for life and build their
nests in bushes, preferring thorny species for protection
from predators. The female does most of the work in
building the nest but the male helps in feeding the young.
Blackbirds are well known for being aggressively territorial
and the males seem to dislike orange-beaked birds on their
patch more than yellow-beaked ones!

Robin
Erithacus rubecula

The iconic robin is one of our most cherished garden birds. Known as the gardeners' friend, the robin will happily perch nearby a person digging the soil, waiting for worms to be unearthed. With its familiar orange breast, the robin was known as 'Robin Redbreast' from the fifteenth century. The robin also features strongly in British folklore and more recently has become an emblem of Christmas. It is likely that it symbolised the delivery of Christmas cards by the red-uniformed postmen, who were known as 'Robins'.

Song Thrush
Turdus philomelos

The song thrush, with its distinctive speckled breast is most
famous (as the name would suggest) for its beautiful voice,
and the melodious musical phrases it produces. However,
the song thrush is not known to be an early riser, and
when the dawn chorus starts at the first light of day, the
song thrush is happy to let the more industrious robin
and blackbird take the first shift, before joining in later.
The song thrush is also a skilled tool user, and will use
a stone as an anvil to break open a snail shell before
enjoying a juicy meal.

Woodpigeon
Columba palumbus

The woodpigeon is one of the largest birds to grace our bird tables. With its portly appearance (mainly feathers!) and waddling gait, its voracious appetite has made it unpopular with farmers, gardeners and bird lovers alike. With a penchant for young shoots and seedlings, it is a major agricultural pest, and it will quickly clear a bird table, leaving lean pickings for smaller garden birds. The capacity of the Woodpigeon's crop is quite astounding – it can store up to 150 acorns!

Starling
Sturnus vulgaris

Starlings are rather noisy, highly sociable birds. While not particularly musical, they are well known as having a talent for mimicry. With their iridescent feathers, starlings are attractive birds but have quite a reputation for being bullies at the bird table, often taking food from smaller species. They have also been known to evict other birds from their nesting sites rather than finding one of their own.

Collared Dove
Streptopelia decaocto

The collared dove is an attractive bird and is such a familiar
sight in our gardens and countryside, it is hard to believe
that it only began to colonise Britain in the 1950s. Its soft,
cooing voice is sometimes mistaken for that of a cuckoo.
Collared doves prefer the company of their mate above all
others and so are often seen in pairs, but will sometimes
form large flocks if food is plentiful. They are, however,
shoddy nest builders, and the twiggy platforms on which
they lay their eggs often collapse and fall to the ground.